SCIENCE POETRY FOR DUMMIES

ARITRA JANA

BALBOA.PRESS

A DIVISION OF HAY HOUSE

Balboa Press books may be ordered through booksellers or by contacting:

Balboa Press
A Division of Hay House
1663 Liberty Drive
Bloomington, IN 47403
www.balboapress.com
844-682-1282

ISBN: 978-1-9822-7814-4 (sc)
ISBN: 978-1-9822-7813-7 (e)

Library of Congress Control Number: 2021924924

Print information available on the last page.

Balboa Press rev. date: 12/15/2021

This book is dedicated to
My Parents
Dr. Malabendu Jana (Ph.D.) and Dr. Arundhati Jana (Ph.D.)

I would like to acknowledge Dr. Nitai Chandra Mondal, Dr. Shree Bhagwan Roy, Dr. Niladri Mondal, Dr. Nandadulal Sannigrahi, Sarat Chandra Jana and Sonali Manna. They have all helped in refining the book.

Prelude

The essence of the poetry is to evoke an imaginative awareness of experience or an emotional response through the symbiosis of language and rhythm. The sounds of the air or the brook can bring an emotional appeal if they are narrated with a magical tune. The beating of the heart has its own rhythm, but the sounds revitalize the beauty of saga of life. All are the magic, but the poetic magic becomes the source of inspiring beauty if it is garnished with the flavor of scientific aroma. The true beauty and the magic of the real world and its exploration becomes an awesome journey if it is revisited in the light of scientific curiosity by the dint of beautiful mind. Aritra-a boy of 12 years with true passionate gifted child has rightly taken an adventure to meet up the thrust of millions for the appetite of the magic of reality and its rediscovery in the lens of curiosity. From anthropology to Zoology, almost all the fields of the scientific domains have been addressed through his passionate appeal with the very delicate poetic appeal. Even, the most modern field of innovation and knowledge of AI have been addressed by the boy of 12 years by the dint of his radiance of knowledge and versatile style.

Aritra has elucidated the wonders of the natural worlds with is incomparable style and inimitable clarity. From DNA to Darwinism or Corona virus to Cancer, the poetic flavor to explain the most difficult unanswered issues have become very simple and lucid by the style of his narrative paintings. Allergies to Asthma, Chloroplasts to cosmology, he has painted the beautiful universe by the dint of his colorful paintings with words embodied with emotion. Archimedes law to Jacob's syndrome or the story of plague to Pascal's law, he has moved hither and thither to draw the attention of the millions although some of the issues are still in a state of flash in the light of the scientific justification. Darwin's great idea is the most important ideas ever to occur to a human mind and the slow but steady changes is the important ingredient in the evolution of life forms. The magical changing of frog into a prince is surely a magic but the magic of reality of evolution from frog to magic and the journey has been explained by this genius with his poetic flavor. Nuclear science is the domain of the college education but the beauty of atoms and the entity of meson, pie, quark etc. have been rightly addressed by this youngster's very simple and lucid language. The unified theory of the physical world has been explained by the beauty of the poem-The string theory. The deep knowledge, exhilarating, magnificent and awesome confidence of the little boy surely deserves a high degree of appreciation for his deep insight to analyze the magic of the reality of nature with the delicate knowledge and bountiful rhythm will surely make the journey inside the title an awesome in general and the youngsters in particular.

Contents

DNA

The blueprint of life,
The recipe of cells,
A deoxyribose
With four elements:
Adenine interacts with thymine with double bonds,
Whereas guanine interacts with cytosine with triple bonds.
Discovered by three,
It has caused the nucleus to be free.
Life depends on it.
Generally, RNAs are single-stranded,
While DNAs are double-stranded.

11 yrs

Darwinism and the Dialectic

From the competition that follows,
As a result of the antagonistic contradictions that fall,
The adaptations that are made are as diverse as a mall.
The adaptations are combined with hunting in a pack
Where communication is on the rack.
With both competition and cooperation,
It is possible for a species to survive,
And they will thrive—
Without which, it is similar to a mouse building a mousetrap
Where the mice are off the map.
The same applies for the adaptations:
The adaptations may end up causing them to not survive.
The new Darwinist idea must extend
Or else it will bend.

13 yrs

Coronavirus

The new variants seeming endless
Is a result of the fact that it can quickly adapt:
It is a raft
That has never sunk.
It has also turned the wave,
With the spike proteins changing
And the new variants ranging,
With some being more severe
As a result of being able to evade the previous known receptors.
By doing so, it has started the process of evolution,
And soon the world will have devolution.
There is the death of neurons
As the symptoms act like pawns.
With the lungs being taken down,
With the overflow of dead cells,
The coronavirus dwells—
Soon, all that has been made is lost.
The cytokine storm is deadlier than the virus itself
And is triggered by the response to the virus;
As it fails to recognize the self.
It ends up doing more damage in the long run.

12 yrs

Diabetes

Excessive blood sugar that starts with insulin resistance,
Where the resistance
Ends up building up over time,
As the body does not want to process that much glucose:
This will eventually desensitize the binding receptors,
Which can end up causing sores.
Later on, with this being the process of prediabetes,
As being overweight becomes the case,
There is a new race.
With this eventually culminating in diabetes,
There is a crash
As the body will start to use fat more often,
Causing weight loss—
Though this loss is at a large cost.
With the other being type 1,
Where the pancreas's function is reduced to none.
As it can no longer produce insulin
Because of an autoimmune reaction,
There is less that gains traction.

11 yrs

Thalassemia

A rare blood disease that affects red blood cells.
This is because not enough hemoglobin is not being produced.
It is genetic and inherited.
This ends up causing anemia.
As it can be as severe as ischemia,
It has the chance to be fatal.
As it is natal,
It can cause great fatigue.
It can cause stillborn babies,
As it has the relative contagion as rabies.
If only one gene is missing, the person is a carrier.
If two genes are missing, it can be mild.
While if three genes are missing, it can be severe.
If all are missing, it is generally fatal.
It may be partially resolved through stem cell treatment in one case.
While in the other, it requires life-long blood transfusion.
Sometimes, only two genes are affected;
Both of those genes regard hemoglobin production.

12 yrs

Huntington's Disease

Nerve cells break down over time in the ganglia.
It is inherited as well.
This can cause amnesia as a result.
Wherein, some behaviors are etched in.
While memory is etched out.
As it causes problems thinking,
It is always fatal.
This is caused by excess glutamine,
Combined with excess amino acids.
Since it is genetic,
It ends up running through families.
The disease is strong as grit,
Since the gene behind it is dominant.

12 yrs

Autism

It is a syndrome that is a group of syndromes,
As it is widespread.
The causes are unknown,
Although the symptoms are shown.
The individual diseases all have similar signs.
It inhibits mental growth,
As well as causing social loath.
It can be mild or severe,
Though its symptoms are always prevalent.
It has the chance to be blatant.
The best treatment as of right now would be to see a psychologist,
Who has the chance to correct some of the behavior caused by autism.

12 yrs

Autophagy

The eating of one's own cells
To replenish with new ones:
This can reverse the effects of aging.
Its effects on the body are drastic,
As it can increase life span.
Autophagy can prevent cancer,
As it eats the cancerous cells through lysosomes.
After it eats, it replenishes with new, noncancerous cells.
One can get autophagy by
Having a diet that is high in fat
But low in carbohydrates,
Which also means eating less sugar.
This is because fat must be converted into energy
That can be used in the body.
Because of this, the body is more efficient at converting fat
To energy that can be used.
Exercise can also trigger autophagy;
Having more exercise can increase your life.

12 yrs

Niemann-Pick Disease

There are three types,
Each with a different cause.
It all comes from
Sphingomyelinase, when it can't
Metabolize fat as well.
Sphingomyelinase is an enzyme
Which plays a crucial role in Niemann-Pick disease.
When there is not enough sphingomyelinase, then
Niemann-Pick disease will eventually occur.
It clogs around many organs,
Such as the spleen and the liver.
The spleen enlarging
can cause the problem of not
having enough platelets,
Which can cause a longer time for
the clotting response to happen,
Including the brain,
And thus it
Can have fatal consequences.

12 yrs

Stroke

There are two types: one
Hemorrhagic, and the other ischemic.
Hemorrhagic strokes occur when there is an aneurysm
Or a weak spot in one of the blood vessels
In the brain, which is usually around
The circle of Willis.
When it bursts, it leaks the blood,
Pressing down on the brain tissue,
Thus causing a stroke where
Lots of brain cells die.
In an ischemic stroke,
The artery gets clogged with plaque,
Which is made from LDL,
Or low-density lipoproteins, which are lipids.
If it ruptures, platelets will try to clot it.
And so it blocks off the artery,
Thus ceasing blood supply to the areas in which
The artery had supplied to.
The effects of a stroke may be deadly,
Though commonly what happens is that
There is numbness on one side, and there also may be
A Headache and also trouble talking.
It has to be treated as soon as possible
Or it can be fatal.
A way to prevent this from occurring
Is to have a healthy life.
This can be treated by a clot buster
Or by a surgery, and psychological
Therapy may be needed afterwards.

12 yrs

Obesity

Can be caused by eating foods
High in sugar and fats.
This can lead to diabetes
Because the liver cannot
Process tons of glucose—
Which is a sugar—
That fast, so it instead
Stores it in body fat,
Where it can be burned later.
Eventually over time,
The liver cannot produce
Enough insulin to meet
The body's demand.
This will cause low blood sugar,
And diabetes can easily
Become permanent with time.
Being obese also increases
The chance of a heart attack and stroke,
As there is more fat
That is converted into excess cholesterol
That will circulate the body.
And if a blood vessel breaks,
Then a clot will form,
But there is a chance
That cholesterol will get trapped in,
Forming plaque which can clog
The section of the artery, minimizing
Or even causing blood flow.

A way to counter obesity
Is to exercise more,
Which will cut down fat.
Obesity has affected much of America.
Soon living standards will degrade.
Make a change now, or never.

12 yrs

HIV

A deadly disease that kills millions
Through wiping the immune system
And then infecting:
Many don't stand a chance.
Without expensive treatment,
Many die.
Many don't know what is happening.
As many are illiterate,
Thinking it's from the air.
No cure,
As many get hit
And it grows and grows.
The fact is that it does not kill by itself;
Rather, it multiplies the self
With the intent of weakening the immune system.

11 yrs

Parkinson's Disease

Known as PD,
It causes degeneration
By the loss of dopaminergic neurons in the nigra.
The second-most frequent neurodegenerative disease—
Few inherit,
While most acquire—
Starts from tremor
To slowness of movement,
With the reason of the genes;
Can be treated with dopamine,
But it will ultimately cause devastation,
And there will be no more deliberation.

11 yrs

Alzheimer's Disease

As it is known as AD,
It is linked to plaque forming.
It is through amyloid-beta and tau.
It will always cause dementia and memory loss.
This is often undetected;
As a result, the disease is further erected.
As most don't know,
It will continue to grow.

11 *yrs*

Cancer

It will cause cells to multiply out of control,
With fatigue, muscle weakness and pain all being outgrowths.
This wouldn't be a problem if it weren't for the competition of resources.
This competition of resources replaces the old cells,
With cancer cells not doing anything useful.
They indirectly kill the remainder of the cells.
Cancer doesn't have a cure; it has a treatment.
However, it is possible to rectify it, given the condition that it is caught early.
And even though the rectification may not exist,
It is better than having a permanently broken wrist.
It is born through a mutation.

13 yrs

Joy

What is good
Can never be seen.
This raises spirit
And lifts the soul
To attitudes
That can only be reached
Through the mind,
The master of all,
An element of the brain
That operates
Through subconscious ways.
This triggers dopamine, serotonin, and epinephrine,
Which are sent
Throughout the body.
From there
You experience joy.

11 yrs

Depression

Depression is caused by sadness,
Though it can quickly end up sliding.
This can cause economic losses,
With mood being largely affected.
Furthermore, this can adversely affect salary loss,
Completing the whole process.
This can be treated by dopamine,
But this is only temporary.
Eventually, much more dopamine will be needed to restore.
Or else, it will be the next lore.

12 yrs

Multiple Sclerosis

As it is known as MS,
It is known by the scars in the CNS.
This is through demyelination.
In other cases, it can be through atrophy of neural axons.
The etiology of the disease is unknown.
It can be caused by environmental or genetic factors.
Which are all redactors.
The inflammation ends up increasing,
With the CNS being completely damaged.
This has no cure;
It only has theraples,
Which will ultimately lead to death.

12 yrs

Prion Diseases

Like scrapie,
To CJD,
It is caused by protein misfolds,
Leads to brain tissue loss,
With memory failure.
As a result,
Problems arise
To near death,
And unknown times.
All that is made is lost.

12 yrs

Classical Conditioning

In psychology,
This is where a neutral stimulus
Is placed with a sensitive one;
Over time it will teach itself,
And it would learn
Many things from it.
It was first proposed
By Ivan Pavlov,
And it developed into
A complex theory
It can explain why some are dearly,
With the others being able to explain how it is possible to persist
Over the others that resist.
It is possible to explain how growth occurs.
As it is based on the original conditions,
And as there are renditions,
It is able to show that it works,
Rather than one that lurks.

12 yrs

Immune System

It is built for defense
For your body
And for its protection.
Built to fight
From viruses to fungi:
With T-cells
To B-cells.
With two types
Adoptive and innate,
It fights until its last breath.

11 yrs

Vaccination

It is made by Jenner,
Who saved many lives.
Through the vaccine,
From smallpox
To polio,
Which are both deadly,
An injection,
Which would last for decades,
With vaccines lasting for centuries,
It is able to preempt the defense of the body.
11 yrs

Loneliness

When singled out,
One feels the effects
Of loneliness.
In their own universe
And isolated,
Within the dark matter
Of space
And the world
One lives in,
One doesn't know what comes next.

11 yrs

Smoking

As it causes many deaths
Relating to the heart
And the lungs,
From arteries
Being restricted
And lungs being black,
It causes swelling and bleeding
To death.

11 yrs

Anxiety

It is not often noticed,
Though can be felt,
With or without
Tears of sorrow
Though the first is rare.
The second
Is usually the case
That ends up happening.
Over and over,
Fast heart rate
Is present;
And to accommodate,
There is rapid breathing
Which go together.
With the heart working
To try keeping up,
They start sweating.
This leads to a red face
As arteries constrict;
And since they are under the skin,
The facial skin
Shows up as red,
Anxiety can be done
With many reasons,
Such as stressed work
And not completing it.
If for many times
This is repeated,
This could lead
To what is undone

Anxiety disorder:
Constant and chronic,
Cannot be changed
Anxiety caused by GABA,
Which is related,
Anxiety leaves
Behind society.
Its effects
Will build up
Overtime and forever.
Though we can change this,
Now or never.

11 yrs

Suicide

The killing of oneself,
It may be caused by
Many reasons, including
The loss of an object
That had satisfied
The person for their life,
To many other reasons.
The best way to treat it
Is by eliminating
The psychological cause.

11Yrs

Life

Made for good
And the contribution
To human society;
Advances such
As general relativity
To quantum physics,
Stem from
The concept
Of existence.

11 yrs

Measles

A disease by a virus,
It can be deadly
And leaves its effects
On the body
For a long time.
It takes time to recover,
With its most visible
One being with the rashes
That are on the skin.
It weakens the immune system
So much that even regular
Ordinary diseases
Such as the flu can kill you.

11 yrs

Turner Syndrome

It affects a female
When an X chromosome
Is missing.
As it causes short stature,
It also causes delays
Into the development into an adulthood.
It is marked by wobbled necks,
As it causes a quarter million cases in the US.
From osteoporosis
To high blood pressure,
It causes mayhem
Which turns into burden
That the victim carries in
Her life forever.

12 yrs

Allergies

As it is caused by hypersensitivity
To a particular substance
Such as peanuts to dust mites,
It occurs with misidentification
The allergic cascade starts when
The allergen and the body come into contact.
The immune system gets stimulated
Following the scheme IgE and antibodies.
Attachment to the allergen and the production of histamine
Results in immediate symptoms.
This will repeat with more exposure.

12 yrs

Immunity

It is adaptive or innate
With specific cells
Which guard the body.
This varies from pathogens
Such as bacteria and viruses
To B-cells which produce antibodies
(Which serves as a marker).
While macrophages kill
Once and for all,
The diseases are as diverse as a mall.

11 yrs

Common cold

It is not just caused
By one virus,
As many replicants exist.
Not many die from it,
Though it is common.
And it can easily
Infect you through contact.
This in most
Cases is not serious,
Though one of the times it is.
It is when you
Have an infection
At around the same time,
Which ends up weakening your immune system.

11 yrs

Heart Attack

It can be caused by the plaque
That builds up in the arteries
Of the heart, specifically the coronary ones.
This will block the artery partially and will end up
Restricting the blood flow to the region of the heart.
This process is known as atherosclerosis;
This results in damaged heart tissue,
Which damages the whole body.
If a blood clot forms around it,
What will happen is that the whole artery
Can be restricted, which means
That the surrounding tissue will fail to work,
Thus, weakening the heart as a whole.
Then from there what will happen,
Is the whole-body will not get enough blood supply,
Causing the body to die as a whole.
Overall, this disease can be fixed
By targeting its causes.

12 yrs

Concussions

Concussions can be deadly and
Imperative to the brain as
Some of the symptoms include
Memory loss or long-term memory impairment.
It can happen in the form of
A whiplash or rotational torque.
In a whiplash,
What happens is that the brain strikes
Against the skull, which sends
Shockwaves throughout the brain.
This results in many large parts of the brain being damaged,
Which can cause many more injuries
Within a day or two.
In a rotational torque,
The body loses consciousness, as
It goes the opposite way
Of the brain stem.

11 yrs

Rhinoviruses

Rhinoviruses are viruses that often
End up causing the cold
And even worse symptoms.
Often called the sister
Of the deadly coronavirus,
This virus replicates
Into different strands
And thus, it is nearly
Impossible to get a vaccination;
However, they are very weak to begin with.

12 yrs

Sickle Cell Anemia

When a mutation
In the DNA
Causes red blood cells
To take the shape
Of a sickle,
It is called sickle cell disease.
By doing so,
The cell has less
Oxygen to bind to,
Making it fatal.
It causes lots of other symptoms.
If not treated,
Its effects can be devastating
To most people.

12 yrs

Jacob's Syndrome

Many problems follow it,
Such as having
Problems mentally and physically.
They tend to be tall
And aggressive.
It can be mistaken
For being mischievous.
While rare, it
Can cause problems
In society and in general.
It is due to genetics,
When the boy has
An extra Y chromosome.

12 yrs

Neuropathy

When the peripheral nerves
Stop functioning properly,
A couple reasons
Are due to diseases
Such as Guillain Barre
And diabetes,
Which accounts for
A good chunk of the cases.
It can cause numbness
And weakness in many places,
Usually in the hands or the feet.

12 yrs

Dengue

It is a fever spread
By many mosquitoes;
As it can kill someone,
It can spread
From a mother
To a child.
It can also be spread
By other insects,
Though a person
May be able to
Recover from it.

12 yrs

Arthritis

It is a complication that
Arises when there
Is pain in the joints.
It can be that the
Joints had worn down
As the person ages
Or it can be for different reasons.
The most common types
Are osteoarthritis and rheumatoid arthritis.
With arthritis, moving
Your joints can be painful and difficult.

12 yrs

Leprosy

It is a disease that is caused by a bacterium.
The name is *Mycobacterium Leprae;*
It tends to happen in countries,
That are close to the equator.
It can spread by direct contact;
It causes many patches on the skin,
And it causes nerve damage,
Which causes numbness in that area.
If left untreated, it can
Cause lots of nerve damage,
And due to that,
It can cause blindness.

12 yrs

Scarlet Fever

It is a fever that effects the throat
And causes many other
Symptoms, combined with that
It can cause a high fever
Along with the throat
Swelling up and
Having dead cells on them.
This turns out to be the color white,
As it causes many rashes
On the person's skin.

12 yrs

Ebola

It causes loss of body fluid
And it causes fever combined
With a severe headache,
Backache, vomiting.
As it is not limited to
Diarrhea and hemorrhaging,
It is transmitted by nature,
But people have
Not figured out how
It is exactly transmitted.

12 yrs

Rotavirus

From diarrhea and vomiting,
It happens in usually children.
It is usually
Found in the
Developing countries of the world.
Its infections are usually self-limiting;
It is usually associated
With severe dehydration
Similar to cholera.
As in order to treat it,
The patient needs to replace
The fluids that were lost.

12 yrs

Rabies

It is a viral disease caused
By a virus named *Rabies lyssavirus*.
In the old world,
They are spread by dogs;
While in the new world,
They are spread by bats.
It can cause a fever
And even a coma.
It is transmitted by a bite;
A vaccine for it was made
By Louis Pasteur.
As, the number of cases had went down in developed countries;
It still remains a problem
In developing countries.

12 yrs

Cholera

It is caused by a bacterium
Named *Vibrio Cholerae.*
It is a diarrheal disease
That is often found
In contaminated water and shellfish,
Which produces a toxin
That upsets the intestine's lining,
As it secretes lots of
Water and electrolytes.
It targets many tropical nations;
And if it is left untreated,
It can cause dehydration and death.

12 yrs

Ulcers

It happens in the stomach,
When the surrounding acid
Is a higher pH
Than the mucus.
As a result, what happens
Is the stomach layer
Breaks apart and the acid
Injures the surrounding tissue —
Which turns very painful.
Doctors do not know
The cause for most cases.

12 yrs

Lyme Disease

A disease that
Is caused by ticks *Borelli bacterium*
And that is why they
Are often despised;
It causes a bullseye
On the skin.
It can also cause facial palsy
And it can cause
A swollen knee.
It can be treated with
Doxycycline and Amoxicillin.

12 yrs

Black Fever

A fever that is caused
By Indian leishmaniasis,
It is a parasite
And it could cause death.
If it remains untreated,
It can also cause a fever,
Loss of appetite,
Fatigue and enlargement
Of two organs:
The liver and spleen.

12 yrs

Trypanosomiasis

A disease caused
By a protozoon,
It enters the body
Through the eyes
Or through breaks
In the skin.
it is very harmful,
As it can also cause
A fever, headache
And weight loss.
And the biggest thing
Is that it causes sleepiness.

12 yrs

Epilepsy

It may occur from a genetic condition
Targeting the CDKL5 gene
Or it may also occur when there is a brain injury;
What it causes is excessive and abnormal brain activity,
Which causes seizures;
Which is an on the moment, uncontrolled electric disturbance
In the brain; this is when considering the fact
That the brain works by using electricity
To transmit signals around the body.
Epilepsy is common with more than 200,000 cases each year
And many medications fail to work against epilepsy.

12 yrs

Migraine

It is a painful headache
That happens many times over;
Some might have an aura
Where they may not be
Able to see or they might
Have imaginary bright spots
Or flashes of light.
With the attack,
The pain occurs even up to 72 hours
Combined with nausea and vomiting.
It is a very painful condition;
Its trigger may be stress;
However, scientists have not been able to find the direct cause.

12 yrs

Asthma

It is caused by genetic and environmental factors,
Especially, by the receptor that is mostly linked to is Interleukin-4
And as for environmental factors, it may be linked
To whatever the patient is allergic to.
Asthma constricts the airways, which is
Located in the upper respiratory system.
Their airways are constricted plus it
Contains mucus, which makes it
Very difficult to breathe with asthma.
It can be treated with either albuterol
Or if it prevents the symptoms,
Then doctors might prescribe steroids.

12 yrs

Traumatic Brain Injury

It is an injury that impacts the brain;
There are many forms such
As a low velocity or sometimes a high
Velocity injury, both with different consequences.
A high velocity one may be fatal
As it impacts it so hard that when the brain
Hits the skull after by passing the cerebellum.
It can cause learning issues and
Difficulty problem solving; it
May be caused by violence;
It can also lead to a coma
And even brain death.

12 yrs

Meningitis

It is the inflammation of brain and the spinal cord;
It may be caused by a bacterial, viral or fungi infection;
As for viruses, it is usually caused by *coxsackie virus A;*
For bacteria, it is usually caused by *Neisseria meningitidis,*
Which spreads through saliva and other respiratory fluids.
The others may be cancer, chemical irritation and drug allergies;
It may cause altered mental status, nausea, vomiting,
Sensitivity to light, purple areas on the skin that resemble bruises,
Sleepiness, lethargy and fevers.
There is a vaccine for meningitis,
Which target the viruses or the bacteria,
Though this lesson may be traumatic.

12 yrs

Transient Ischemic Attack

An attack that is also called a mini stroke
Because for a short amount of time,
The artery is blocked because of plaque
Which eventually builds up.
As it may have lots of cholesterol and fat,
That may get lodged,
For a short amount of time.
It takes a professional
To distinguish it from a regular stoke.
It can cause drooping of the face,
As the biggest thing is to
Seek medical assistance right away.

12 yrs

58

Addiction

When a drug is used over and over,
The receptors end up urging the consumption of those drugs;
This is directly linked to the use of the drug,
Which only turns out to be addictive as a result of receptors binding.
It may be a result of many reasons, including to boost performance,
All the way to increase how many endorphins are released.
As the mood is elevated temporarily,
It is important to realize the side effects which end up escalating it.
The increase in performance is for the facilitation of a high.
This would mean the near instant gratification from the drug.
As it serves with its own mug,
It is able to sweep the harm under the rug.

11 yrs

Hypnosis

When a person has insane
Amounts of concentration
On one thing,
Its psychological effects are revealed.
As the person becomes subconscious,
Which is conscious but not fully,
Then the person is hypnotized.
It can be serious,
As the person will not know
What is happening in front of
Himself or herself.

12 yrs

Pica

From eating ice
To eating paper
And to eating anything
That should be inedible,
This is an eating disorder
That can cause damage
To the human body
And it is very serious;
Its cause may be
A lack of iron,
Which can also cause anemia.

11 yrs

CJD

A rare disease that
Can kill a person,
It starts with altered prions
And in some variants,
It is linked to BSE —
Which comes from eating contaminated beef.
In other cases, it is sporadic
And the cause is never known,
And within a few months
The patient will die.
The initial onset of symptoms
Takes 28 years.

11yrs

Lassa Virus

This is transmitted
Via mice and this can
Cause a hemorrhage in the body.
This means the body will
Bleed itself either from
The outside or even worse,
From the inside.
This is very prevalent in West Africa;
This can be treated with Ribavirin;
This can be found using antigen
Markers while testing.

12 yrs

Stress

It is a psychological condition,
In which it overtakes a person mentally;
It ends up having the chance of harming them physically.
It can cause many symptoms ranging from nervousness,
All the way to shaking.
It can be combined with many other symptoms,
Which all contribute to a person's ability to do things.
It can be treated by the self,
For using something else would require pelf.

11 Yrs

Oxidative Stress

An imbalance between the systemic manifestations
Of reactive oxygen species,
It can cause many diseases such
As ADHD, Cancer and myocardial infarction;
One way to counter this is to eat antioxidants
Such as artichokes, raspberries and kale;
Severe cases can cause the cell to die;
Thus, this will age the body.
And it can cause neurodegenerative diseases
Such as Parkinson's and Alzheimer's Disease;
It can cause death,
Which is why a healthy lifestyle will help.

11 yrs

Heart Failure

This occurs when the heart does not pump enough blood
That the body needs, depriving tissues
Of oxygen in the blood.
Thus, the tissue around the heart weakens;
Some have a pump regulator
To help the heartbeat normally;
Some others have a transplant
And use the donor's heart instead.
This is because the other one is dysfunctional
And it would not work as a result.

12 yrs

Schizophrenia

As it can vary from seizures to hallucinations in teens,
It is often not noticed;
As many of the problems are likewise;
In adults, it is noticeable because it may cause a different reality;
It is mainly treated with psychotherapy and supportive care,
Though sometimes drugs may be used.
This can cause the old problem to be amused.

12 yrs

Typhoid

It can cause many symptoms;
It is caused by *Salmonella Typhi*,
Which is a bacterium.
It can cause high fever,
Stomach pains
And diarrhea.
This can make it a complication,
As many organs
May start of ache.
As it spreads to nearby tissue,
It causes another issue.
This may be treatable;
Though when it is left alone,
It is like multiple people vying for the throne.
It causes the same problem in the end;
There is no real difference as the others bend.
All that has changed for the rest
Is minimal; however, the major functions
Are hampered as there is only one junction.

12 yrs

Tapeworm

They are parasites with no
Gut or mouth.
It comes from food,
As they eat away
At the guts.
It can be deadly
When they reach the brain;
It is as if it eats away at that.
A person can take
Severe brain damage;
It is similar to a rampage.
Though this is one that affects the mastermind,
As it severely weakening the rest.
It imitates a false guest.

12 yrs

Hepatitis

When the liver is
Infected by this virus,
Many cells die.
It inflames
As it grows larger and larger,
As it occupies more.
These cells
Do not work anymore.
Thus, the liver
Is essentially destroyed.
And as the regeneration capability takes longer,
It can cause the rest to not render.
With the result depending
On which type it is,
It is like a ring.
This time, it is lost.
It has a harder chance of going back,
As it sits on the rack.

12 yrs

Muscular Dystrophy

A disease which
Stems from abnormal genes,
It can cause inefficient protein building.
The results vary from progressive weakness,
To loss of muscle mass.
It can also cause learning disabilities
And frequent falls.
It can cause breathing problems,
Which forces the use of a ventilator.
It can cause heart issues,
Most notably reducing the efficiency.
It is mainly treated with steroids,
Though they do not last forever,
But it is better than never,
Whose consequences are much greater
And it will delay the rest until later.

11 yrs

CKD

Can be caused by diabetes,
But it can also be caused
By high blood pressure.
And what happens
Is the kidney starts to
Dysfunction and due to that,
What happens is anemia
And nausea along
Side with fluid retention.
As the kidneys cannot function properly,
It must be combated early;
Or else, it will end up with none
That exists in the end.
And soon, the others will bend.

12 yrs

COPD

It can be caused by
Smoking but it can also
Be caused by other factors.
It can cause lung cancer
And high blood pressure.
In the lung arteries,
It causes chest tightening
Combined with a chronic
Cough which causes mucus
To be coughed out.
And there is no doubt
That the results are long-lasting,
As the malicious are blasting.

12 yrs

PTSD

When a traumatic
Experience happens over
Someone's lifetime and
It keeps recurring within
Their memory it
Becomes PTSD, which
Brings along lots
Of other symptoms
That can recur
Within someone's lifetime
And haunt them forever.
As it can recur,
It can incur
With the repeat remaining
And with the momentum gaining.

12 yrs

Wilson's Disease

It is a rare genetic
Disease, in which the
Body cannot get rid of copper.
And so, it accumulates in the body.
It can cause an eye
Discoloration, with it being golden-brown.
It causes fluid buildup and jaundice;
It also causes uncontrolled movements.
It also causes stiffness.
Lastly, it can cause liver cirrhosis.

12 yrs

Familial Fatal Insomnia

It is a hereditary disease that
Affects the hippocampus.
It ends up killing the cells due
To misfolded prions and
So, the person cannot
Sleep which overtime
Will lead to deaths and
As with other prion diseases,
There is no cure and
The prognosis is absolute.

11 yrs

Hemophilia

It can be caused by genes
Such as factor VIII or
It can be caused
By factor IX.
However, it can also be caused
By cancer or autoimmunity,
It causes large and
Deep bruises including
Excessive bleeding and arthritis,
If internal bleeding occurs.

11 yrs

Rickets

It Can be genetic or
It Can be caused by a
Vitamin D deficiency, which
Causes the bones to be weak.
As a result, they can
Easily be fractured from there on.
It can cause delayed growth
And delayed development of
Motor skills which are essential.
However, it can be treated by Vitamin D supplements.
If it is genetic,
It can be hectic,
Which would be an understatement in itself.
It is similar to not paying rent,
With the consequences in the end,
That never bend.
With the delayed development,
It can cause a dent
That lasts a lifetime,
And one that continues to rhyme.

12 yrs

Coats' Disease

It is a disease that is present
From birth, though it is not
Hereditary. it
Leads to blindness in
The eye that is affected.
With other symptoms including
Pink eye, due to inflammation.
It is gradual,
Which makes it so that
The first signs could be from
Five months to seventy-one years.
It is like those deer
Which have been hunted down.
With the signs showing up within those times,
It can cause the others to rhyme.
When the initial symptoms are there,
The battle is not fair.

12 yrs

Septicemic Plague

It is caused by *Yersinia Pestis.*
However, the symptoms are different because
It occurs when the bacteria
Rapidly multiplies along your
Bloodstream. Some symptoms
Include blackening and death of tissues,
Mainly at the digits, combined
With extreme weakness
And that is combined with shock.
All of these make death inevitable
Without any treatment.
This is with the testament
Of the last person that has been there.
Without the treatment,
It can cause a dent;
As it leaves destruction behind it,
It causes rent.

11 yrs

Bubonic Plague

It is the most common plague
Out of all of them.
The bacteria behind it
Is *Yersinia pestis.*
It is caused by rats as
They transmit them to
Humans and the symptoms
That develop are swollen lymph nodes.
These are called buboes and
They are situated on the neck.
They are typically the size
Of chicken eggs,
As they end up in the legs.
The bubonic plague has brought the largest row comparatively
And it is one of the darkest.

11 yrs

Pneumonic Plague

Caused by *Yersinia Pestis,*
It is the most dangerous,
As it can be spread from person to person
Through droplets. Because
It causes Sputum combined
With difficulty breathing and nausea,
It can ultimately lead
To death, which is why
Medical care is urgently needed.
Otherwise, the patient can end up dying,
As it ends with the story of rye.
Soon, the plague will go further
And the world will murmur.

11 yrs

Sleep

It is characterized by relative unconsciousness
And reduced body movement.
It has four stages
That lead to dreams.
With chemical messengers
Maintaining alertness,
Some disorders exist
With insomnia,
Which does not give quality sleep,
On and on.
Insomnia is one of a disorder
Which can prevent order
When it is expressed later on.

11 yrs

Emotion

It consists of psychological and cultural factors
Responding to stimuli.
The amygdala is used;
Some are complex,
While others are simple.
The endocrine system is one.
By the nervous system,
Sensation caused by arousal,
Responding to the surrounding,
Which triggers the senses
And each of them has their own lenses.

11 yrs

Filariasis

It is caused by *Wuchereria bancrofti*.
Which is a parasite and a
Symptom is the swelling of the skin
Of a leg, which makes the leg much
Larger and the patient cannot walk.
Soon, the pain will be intense
To the point that they cannot talk.
It enters through a mosquito
And then once the mosquito bites,
The human, the parasite reproduces
And it spreads to the blood vessels,
Causing swelling from there.

12 yrs

Environmental Standards

These regulations should be put
In place over time so factories
Can be adjusted to fit these accommodations.
The etymology behind doing so
Is very simple, which is
Preserving the environment for humanity.
If we can do so, then the carbon
Dioxide in the air will soon drop;
And as it will drop, the air will
Become cleaner and Antarctica and the Arctic
Will be preserved as the temperature on
Average goes down. whether other
Nations will be ignorant can
Be solved by building everything in our economy
And flooding the market so the price of goods
Will go down, thus making their economy take
A huge toll as it refuses to comply
To the standards of environment that
Should be set; Not
Only that, it will lower the amount
Of people that die from respiratory illnesses.

12 yrs

The Super Bacteria

As it is unstoppable,
It is not permeable.
The super bacteria were born out of the antibiotics.
As it was born out of it,
It has the strength of grit.
The super bacteria is able to rapidly multiply.
As it has adapted against the antibiotics,
This is the path we are going down
And this is a direct result of the gown
Which ends up hiding the true nature
Of the current state of industrial farming.
Where antibiotics are used in close quarters,
This is not only a medical problem;
This is a problem of economics as well.
For it is a result of the close quarters where the animals dwell,
Which has also displaced many of the family farms in the past.

13 yrs

Giardiasis

This causes diarrhea
And this can be spread
By contaminated food.
Other symptoms include
Dehydration and weight loss
And this may not also
Cause symptoms at all.
This can be treated
With prescription drugs;
This disease is typically not fatal.

12 yrs

Sepsis

This is what happens
When the body reacts
In an extreme way.
Sepsis can lead to death,
If emergency care isn't given.
Any infection can cause
Sepsis and this will
Also lead to multi-organ failure.
Symptoms include a high heart rate
And extreme pain.

12 yrs

Mitosis

It is part of the cell cycle.
It has a couple of phases,
Including the Interphase, Prophase
Prometaphase, Metaphase, Anaphase
And Telophase; afterwards,
Cytokinesis occurs and
The end result
Of Mitosis is cell division
And the formation of a new
Cell, which will eventually reproduce
And this is part of where the produce
Comes from.

12 yrs

Meiosis

Having many stages
Including Prophase I
And Prophase II,
Meiosis is a special
Type of division
In which germ cells
Reproduce; in humans,
This will create
An embryo in the end.
Meiosis is the result
Of the reproduction of germ cells;
Soon, they will dwell.

12 yrs

Telomeres

Telomeres dictate how
Long a cell can multiply.
The more the cell multiplies,
The more the telomeres
Shorten and this can
Practically determine the life
Of a person somewhat; if
The telomeres shrink enough,
In other words, aging, then
What will happen is that
The cell might stop multiplying.

12 yrs

Inflammatory Bowel Disease

This includes Crohn's Disease
And Ulcerative Colitis.
This will typically cause
Bloody stools and
Crohn's disease; Crohn's disease is possibly
Caused by an immune system
That isn't properly working.
The tissues are
Damaged in inflammatory
Bowel disease and that's
What causes blood to leak.

11 yrs

Dog Heartworm

This is a parasite
That is transmitted
Via mosquito bites
And they cause
Granulomas, which are
Small nodules and they
Are caused by the inflammatory
Response to dying parasites.
These granulomas happen in
The pulmonary artery branches;
This can cause chest pain
And coughing up blood.

12 yrs

Bladder Cancer

This typically causes
Blood in urine and
This is the result of
The cells of the bladder
Multiplying out of control.
This is because they no longer
Have a signal which
Says that they should stop
Multiplying, combined with
This having a chance
To spread to other organs.

12 yrs

Schistosomiasis

This disease is
Caused by multiple
Parasites and contaminated
Fresh water with snails can
Cause the disease.
This typically causes
Chills and a fever.
But if it makes
It to the brain, then
This can cause
Seizures and paralysis.

12 yrs

Deep Vein Thrombosis

This is when a blood
Clot forms in a deep vein.
This can stop blood
From reaching the lungs
And this is fatal.
If this is small
However, the patient
Can recover from it.
Many will not have
Symptoms but this is life threatening.

12 yrs

Shingles

It is the reinfection
Of chickenpox once
The virus becomes inactive.
This can cause
Fevers, headaches
And rashes but
This can also cause
Death combined with
The inflammation of the brain.
This can cause pneumonia
And hearing problems.

12 yrs

Microcephaly

This is when
A baby's head is
Much smaller than normal.
This can cause
Mental challenges, seizures,
Hearing loss, problems with
Eyesight and it can
Make it difficult
To swallow something.
This means that
The baby's brain
Didn't develop properly.

13 yrs

Cestoda

All of the species
Are parasites and
They absorb the host's nutrients,
Being able to somewhat starve the host.
Immunity can develop from
This, as antibodies may
End up coming if the wall
Of the host if it is damaged.
This will not happen
If the parasite does it
Without damaging the host.

13 yrs

Anotia and Microtia

This is when
The part of the ear
That can be seen
Is completely missing
Or it is small in size.
This may also
Affect the middle ear,
Which can cause more problems.
This ranges from 1 through 4
In severity and this can
Cause death at times.

13 yrs

Chromosomes

It is found in cells
With 23 pairs,
It can dictate syndromes
Such as down syndrome.
As there are 3 of 21,
Rather than 2,
This will cause a syndrome.
Doubles exist
To have a replacement copy.
It can dictate gender
With XX for female
And XY for male.
Less complex organisms
May have more or less.
Some cells do not have chromosomes.
Even though there can be exceptions
With some being redone,
There is almost never a such thing as none.

11 yrs

Chloroplasts

It makes up plant life
As it is.
It collects energy from the sun
Via photosynthesis,
Whose output is glucose,
Which the plant uses
To support itself.
The cyanobacteria are ancestors;
That make up plant diversity.
With their original function being separated,
They would soon be integrated.

10 Yrs

Mitochondria

It gives energy
To the cells
Which process life
As it is.
It uses ATP, as they are
The direct ancestors of bacteria.
It provides the cell
With what it needs
To function
And to grow.
It is always used by cells;
It is an integral part of the system.

10 yrs

Pain and Pleasure

It is something that is experienced through a signal up the spine.
It is one that is similar to wine.
It can be altered by painkillers.
These are also known as NSAIDS.
This blocks sensations, with anesthetics.
If they are cut off, the inhibition could be stopped,
Though this would require opioids.
The rest will alter the amount that is needed,
With the rest being heeded.

12 yrs

Memory

It is to recall
And to know.
It goes through the hippocampus
And gets absorbed.
It comes in two types,
Short and long.
With short-term memory being
Used for minutes,
And long used for years.
It is also stored in the amygdala.
With amnesia
Prevalent
After a head injury,
Combined with memory loss,
The loss is amplified.
Its difference is the difference between many animals and humans,
As some other animals can recall.

12 yrs

Vaccines

As dead or weakened pathogens are injected into the bloodstream,
Antibodies form in the body.
As the B Cells mark one,
They are treated like the actual.
Thus, the fake is destroyed;
The fake is also remembered.
When the real ends up coming,
It is easily destroyed.
It is similar to a human killing an ant.
As the immunity is being given with new exposure.

11 yrs

Viruses

As it is dead but deadly,
It uses the host cell's resources,
Wherein it ends up hijacking the cell.
From there, it turns alive.
Some are single while others are double stranded.
They cannot be killed by antibiotics.
They use the host cell machinery.
Which they harness into a factory.
This overstresses it and then, it kills it.
It begins a disease.
It causes rabies and the flu.
As if the immune system knew,
But couldn't act as a result of not being specific.

11 yrs

Mendels Laws

With those coming from evolution
A couple of laws end up coming into play,
Wherein there is the law of dominance.
The law of dominance is one of the fittest taking over.
With one going left and one going right.
It is always varying;
The last is one where both parents contribute;
As a result, one becomes dominant.
With Mendel's Laws,
Each has their own modified paws.

11 yrs

Evolution

Many reproduce while the genetic changes occur.
As a result, adaptations occur,
Which end up allowing for changes inside.
This is because in order to keep up,
Natural selection ends up occurring.
This is where fittest are selected.
With part of the offspring remaining alive,
While the rest end up dying.
This is the fate that those that didn't adapt face.
It is one of extinction, while those that did adapt will reproduce more.

10 yrs

Enzymes

With the goal of bringing about a specific biochemical reaction,
It is one that is able to gain traction.
This is on top of bring about process the other chemicals.
This is with the intent of being able to change them so the cells can use them.
As they are a gem
When there are not as many,
There is a new decay.
As it is directly important for life,
Without which, there would be strife.
For example, without them,
They will act like a gem.

12 yrs

Hormones

They are the building block
Of many of the processes to make,
Rather than to take.
Hormones are necessary
Because without which,
What would end up happening is that the human species could not replicate
And this would mean to the end of humans.
They are there to signal
With the general changes that are made
And the plan laid.
The goal of them is to make them do a certain action,
Rather than have retraction.

12 yrs

Soil

It is used for farming;
It is separate from dirt.
Like water,
Society cannot function without it.
It supports plant life
To animal life.
It is the basic need
And it is organic.
It is from nature;
It indirectly influences the economy
Through agriculture.
It is important to conserve
For fertility.
Farmers need to use rotation.
Soil is equal to life;
Without which, there will be strife.

11 Yrs

Physics

The foundation of knowledge
From mass
To space and to time.
Physics explains everything,
Machines are built
On the basis of physics
To radiation
And to the light
That we see.
These all make up what physics is
And as some is done with glee.
In reality, most is unknown
And not much is shown.
As still, there is a galaxy ahead
Before it is possible to chase the bread.
And soon, we will head
To our own distinct part,
Before it is a cart
That brings us down
To the path of unknowns.

11 yrs

Quantum Physics

Known for its dual existence,
It is one of the main
Of the two subjects
Of modern physics
Along with general relativity.
It explains virtually anything
That is in the universe.
It is the theory of atoms.
It is more accurate
As it used for precision.
It started ancient,
Though it was modern
With the plum pudding model.
Much more was known
When a photon can be a wave.
It can also be a particle
As it can be a trickle.
It can power the next evolution;
It can cause devolution.

11 yrs

Energy

It is measured in Joules.
It has different types,
Such as kinetic.
The energy of motion
Creates thermal energy.
Some are radiant,
Such as once caused by nukes.
Perpetual motion cannot exist,
Due to friction.
This causes machines to lose energy.
Nuclear energy is a larger scale
And a slightest spark
Could cause death for humanity,
With the rest acting like it is a park.
In reality, it must be avoided at all costs.
No cow would build a slaughterhouse,
Yet we did
And we hid.

9 yrs

Magnet

It causes fields
To attract.
With some being massive,
Such as the Earth's.
It causes compasses to work,
Which helps with navigation
To modern GPS.
The unlike attract
While the like repel.
Electromagnets work
Which explains the direction
And this could be applied to the pen
That is able to be pulled away
And is forced to have its pay.
With the magnet being able to sway
And it shines a light like a ray.

11 yrs

Force

It was explained by Newton
With his second law.
In which, it is stated that force is directed
By mass
Times acceleration.
It can be as basic as a push
To a pull.
In advanced fields,
Such as machines moving
Friction where uneven collide
To lubrication which stops it.
The force that shines
Is one that rhymes.
With the force being one that can transform,
Rather than reform.
As it is able to change the direction,
Force is what drives any change in speed
With force being able to move any object;
It is able to reject.

11 yrs

Nuclear science

With fission and fusion,
Which end up drawing against each other,
They all share the same mother.
This is one of the facts that they originate from nucleus,
Where they will merge into one
Or they will merge into none;
Rather, dividing into two.
There is no more plight,
When it comes to the individual level,
Though when it comes to the collective.
This time, before it is taken from the Earth,
It is much greater.

11 yrs

Cosmology

It is the explanation of space and more.
Known for space time
To life and death,
It explains multiverses
To the universe.
This includes fine-tuning,
Explaining all of the phenomena.
It includes formulas made by Einstein
Including the Big Bang.
Quantum gravity is included,
Explaining cosmology
Once and for all.
And with the discovery,
Came with the recovery.
It was the recovery of knowledge
And it would cause some to pledge
To the idea of life elsewhere
And soon, the table would be fair.

11 yrs

States of Matter

Solids are the most ordered;
While some are fragmented,
Others are brittle.
Others are ductile
As it melts.
Liquids may become viscous,
While some have low viscosity.
At a higher temperature,
Where water evaporates at 373 K
And no bonds form.
While the rest break,
What is remaining is a gas
As it shares the same mass,
Even at last.

9 yrs

Rotational Motion

It is a beauty of nature,
As it describes the interactions with objects.
It is known for simplicity
As it describes motion.
With the famous law,
Force is equal to mass times acceleration,
With the momentum being mass and velocity together;
It is also used to describe rotational motion,
Always revolved around torque,
Which describes motion while turning
And motion with rotational force.
It describes and explains common habits;
It is the language of the universe
And it creates a new verse,
In which some can submerse.

12 yrs

The other multiverse

The other multiverse is one where the current laws cease
With the opposition being met with a decrease.
The other multiverse develops over time
With the multiverse being able to rhyme.
There will soon be a chime
With the other multiverse.
Expanding far beyond our current reach
And once we go onto the beach,
The other multiverse will break many of our laws.
Potentially including gravity,
With the other multiverse
Showing a new consistent definition
That is far beyond our heads.

12 yrs

The Exploration of Mars

With the exploration of Mars,
It is as big as the advent of cars.
With the exploration being able to create,
With the new procreation,
It leads to a new age,
With the new era.
It is able to bring forth new discoveries,
In one where gravity no longer exists.
The concept of spacetime ceases to exist too.
The exploration of the other galaxies
And the eventual exploration of a multiverse
Will allow for space and time's chains to be broken.
And soon, they will both cease to exist.
Once the atom is liberated from the multiverse,
The laws that define it will be changed
With the old laws being deranged.

13 yrs

M theory

It unifies superstring theory
And explains the universe.
Particles are replaced
By strings in string theory,
As it attempts to bypass
The problem of quantum gravity
By replacing particles with strings.
And thus, by doing so,
It tries to explain everything
In the universe.
And as it has some girth,
It is able to get the ball rolling
In the new idea that it is universal,
Rather than act like a rehearsal.

13 yrs

D Branes

Its use is in the study
Of black holes and black
Holes have entropy;
It is used in figuring
Out if black holes
Have entropy.
D branes are a part of
String theory which explains
All of the universe.
Black holes need to keep
The second law of thermodynamics, which
Is the point of this.

13 yrs

String Theory

It explains everything in
The universe, though
It uses strings instead
Of the points.
It also uses
The brane to represent
The theory behind it.
It is a merger
Between two different theories.
It also makes
It so that
Gravity can coexist
Along with quantum theories
That had previously existed.
Black holes exist
Within this theory.

12 yrs

Quarks

It is an elementary particle;
Quarks are subatomic
And quarks have 6 types.
They have fractional;
It is electoral charges times
The elementary charge
And thus, this means
That the elementary
Charge is being
Multiplied by a fractional number.

12 yrs

Amonton's law

This is the pressure of
The gas divided
By the temperature
Of the gas is equal
To k, which is a constant.
And this means
That the ratio
Between the pressure
Of a gas of a fixed mass
And volume is equal to
The gas' absolute temperature.

12 yrs

Avogadro's Law

This is the volume of gas
Divided by the
Amount of substance that
Is in it and this
Is in the form of moles.
It is equal to a constant
That is there for
A given temperature
And pressure and this
Is derived from the ideal gas law.

11 yrs

Linear Motion

It is a one directional motion
And it is a vector.
Linear motion means
Finding the displacement
Of one object, finding
The velocity, the acceleration
And lastly, finding the jerk
Of the object; linear
Motion is useful in telling
How something moves.

12 yrs

Vibration

It consists of oscillations occurring where
The equilibrium point is,
As the vibrations range
From a simple spring
To drums and vibrations.
They have three types,
Free, forced and damped.
These three are distinct
From each other.
Vibrations exist everywhere in physics.

12 yrs

Simple Harmonic Motion

It is given by force
Is equal to the negative
Spring constant times
The displacement from
The equilibrium positions
And this is equal to
The restoring elastic
Force; this
Is a type
Of periodic motion.

12 yrs

Space

It is boundless
And it is a key
Principle of physics.
As space is three
Dimensions, it
Relates to relativity.
And it is three
Dimensions as long
As time is not included,
Which makes it so
That space hosts
Objects that are relative to it.

12 yrs

Reflection

This is what happens when
Light bounces off
The object rather
Than being absorbed.
And thus, reflection
Is based on
What the object is
And if it allows light
To bounce off or
If there is a chance
That it gets reflected.

12 yrs

Refraction

It is when light passes
Through one medium,
With some of the
Light being absorbed
By whatever is underneath.
Refraction makes it
So that if the light
Hits at a certain angle,
It will cause a reflection
At the same angle.

12 yrs

Pascal's law

When there is a change somewhere among the fluid,
There is a change elsewhere as it gets rid
Of the change to make sure that there is a balance in
The change in pressure when it comes to the liquid.
And as there is a lid,
Some of the pressure is changed again.
Pascal's law means that the change
In the pressure causes a different range.
And this is important for general use,
Especially when it comes to lifting
And when it comes to pressing.
Their devices follow this principle
Or else, it will fail
Like a train that goes off the rail.

12 yrs

Technology

It progresses over time
With new inventions
Such as
Nuclear physics
And biotechnology.
Scientists are the ones
Behind this
Though sometimes beneficial
In cases,
The nuclear bomb will be destructive
To mankind and civilization
Itself,
That humans have built
With sweat, toil and blood.

11 yrs

Geothermal Energy

It can produce lots
Of energy while
Still saving the environment,
Which makes it very efficient.
And it makes
It so civilization will last
And when it can be readily available,
It should be implemented.
When the majority can
Afford it, then
The malicious ones can be outlawed.

12 yrs

Ionic Bonding

It is one that has a charge
Of negative one;
It bonds to some
With cations.
It is based on the octet rule
Including anions
With carrying charges.
As both need to have an outer shell,
There needs to be a full outer shell
Where the closest is rounded.
For a full shell,
Some will repel
While others will dwell.

11 yrs

Space Exploration

It should be encouraged as
Whoever gets there first will
Have an unlimited number of resources, which
In turn the nation that had explored
Will have a monopoly in raw materials;
Thus, they could control the
Supply of the world market whenever
They want to punish an opponent
Which makes space exploration valuable.
And thus, it could be a trillion-dollar industry.

12 yrs

Inorganic Compounds

They do not form
Bonds with hydrogen.
And this sets
Them apart from organic
Compounds as organic compounds
Do form bonds with hydrogen.
Many of them are
Minerals and many
Are oxides such as
Carbon monoxide;
This makes inorganic compounds
Different from organic compounds.

11 yrs

Pi

Pi times r squared is the area of a pie.
Half of a pie is ½ πr^2.
A pie sliced up into eight pieces is 1/8 πr^2.
The diameter of the pie is 2r.
Pi is used in everywhere;
It is pi,
Which can make some cry
And can make some dry.

8 yrs

Black Hole

It is where no light can escape.
It was discovered by Einstein
And made real by Frankenstein.
It is faster than the speed of light
With all its might.
A black hole is a wormhole
But it also has to play its role
And as it has transformed with a hole,
There is no longer a single goal.

10 yrs

Relativity

It was made by Einstein,
Stating $E = mc^2$.
It was made of energy
For the purpose of how space and time relate.
If not, locations would be wrong.
It fails at black hole,
But stands up against everything else.
As it was in opposition to that,
The black hole acted like the rat
Where it failed,
Until there was a new one that was railed.

11 yrs

Electromagnetic waves

It is produced by radioactivity.
It can kill cancer
With gamma.
And X-rays, X-rays are able to pass through soft tissue.
Some are absorbed
To the sun,
Which produces ultraviolet.
We can partly see and
Succeeded by infrared,
Which is below.
And to cooking, which emits microwaves,
Which ends in radio waves
With the different waves.
There were different raves.
As it goes by,
It does not cry.

11 yrs

Jerk

It is the third derivative of
Position and jerk;
It is the second derivative of
Velocity and the first
Derivative of acceleration.
Any derivative past
Jerk appears rarely
In real life.
Jerk is sudden and
Unlike acceleration, it isn't
Over some time; it is sudden
Like a car brake.

12 yrs

Displacement

It is the shortest distance
Between the start point
And the end point when
An object moves; and this
Is different from the distance,
As the distance can be increasing
While the displacement
Won't be increased.
Displacement is a vector;
It thus, has a direction,
Unlike a scalar.

11 yrs

Pressure and volume

As pressure goes down,
Volume goes up.
And likewise, the
reverse is true.
This is derived from
Boyle's law and pressure.
It is directly dependent
On the volume of
A substance and thus,
The two are correlated.
They both influence each other.

12 yrs

Work

Work in physics represents force times distance,
Which means that the object is being worked on.
This is represented through W = Fd.
Work is dependent on force and distance;
As for any change in position,
There must be a force behind it,
With the force having grit.
Otherwise, what would happen is that the work would be cancelled,
And nothing will be propelled.
Thus, work must have a force behind it.
The force must be able to counteract the other forces.
For it is able to speed up the horses,
That end up carrying the work.

11 yrs

Faraday's law

This law is
Used in electromagnetism
And it states
The electromotive force
That is around a closed path
Is equal to the
Negative of the rate of change
When it comes to time
Of the magnetic flux
That is enclosed by the path.
And as there is one that is enclosed by the wrath,
Faraday's law persists
As it also resists,
With the change
Being those within a range.

12 yrs

Elastic Energy

It is the potential
Energy that is mechanic
And elastic energy
Is stored when the mechanical
System is deformed
When force is applied.
Elastic energy comes in many forms.
This includes stretching,
Bending, twisting, shearing
And turning which
All distort the material.

12 yrs

Potential Energy

Energy that is held
By an object is potential energy.
This can
Become kinetic energy
If it is used.
Potential energy exists
When you hold down a spring.
Potential energy later on
Becomes kinetic energy.
Potential energy
Is also there when you hit
Keys on a keyboard and then
The potential energy becomes kinetic energy.

12 yrs

Archimedes Law

The up thrust of a body inside of a fluid,
Is always equal to the weight of the fluid,
That the body ends up displacing.
This does have an exception of complex fluids,
Wherein the law ends up failing.

11 yrs

Universal Gravitation

Universal gravitation is everywhere in the universe.
As it applies to everything in the universe,
It is a constituent part of the universe.
The universe wouldn't have the verse,
If it weren't present.
The force is equal to the product of multiple instruments:
The gravitational constant, the mass of objects,
As well as the reciprocal of the distance from the center of the mass.
Gravity is everywhere.

11 yrs

Galaxy Cluster

Galaxy clusters are federations of galaxies.
They are bound together by gravity.
Which have their own brevity.
They are held together,
However, they are moving away from each other.
They are losing their mother,
Which consists of gravity.
The force is becoming weaker and they are moving away as a result.

12 yrs

Dark Energy

As an unknown form of energy,
It is able to defeat the old anti-scientific clergy.
It affects the universe,
When it comes to the largest scale.
As everything stands in pale.
It constitutes majority of the universe.
It is larger than dark matter,
As it has unknown properties.
This leads to the last point where it is an unknown form of energy.

12 yrs

Virtual Machine

It can be used to run
Critical IT Infrastructure or
Host a website, though
They are much less efficient
As they will end up using
More resources than a container
As it will have a separate kernel which
Makes it so that the system
Will have to run two at the same time.
And due to that, it may be unattractive.

12 yrs

Aerodynamics

It is the study of the motion
Of air when it is
Affected by a solid object.
There are three
Principles of conservation,
Which are the conservation
Of mass, momentum
And energy; These
Forces interact in order
To form the basis
Of the study of aerodynamics.

11 yrs

Speed

Speed is either
The average speed
Over time or it is
The instantaneous speed.
Speed can be calculated through
The average for the average
Speed; For the instantaneous speed,
It can be calculated by taking the derivative,
Which itself is looking
For a tangent line on a curve
And the tangent line only.
It intersects at one point, thus
Giving the answer.

12 yrs

Anions and Cations

An anion has
More electrons than
Protons and thus
It has a negative
Charge compared to
A cation, which has
A positive charge.
A cation has a positive charge
As a result of having
More protons than electrons.

11 yrs

Inertia

It is the resistance posed
By an object to
A change in velocity.
It is the resistance
To it and this
Also includes the direction
Of motion and speed
Of which it is resistant to.
This is because the direction
Of motion and speed make
Up the velocity, thus it
Is also resistant to those too.

12 yrs

Euler's first law

This applies to
Rigid body motion
And Euler's first
Law explains how
The linear momentum
Is equal to the mass
Of the body times
The velocity of its
Center. thus, this means
That mass times
The velocity of the center
Is equal to the linear momentum.

12 yrs

Impulse

It is the integral
Of force over time.
J is the integral
Of F over the initial time
To the end time.
Impulses include a golf
Shot for example, where
Force is applied
Within the initial
Time to the end time.

12 yrs

Scale

There are many
universal laws.
However, some of these
Laws may not be
Applicable, since it
Is based on scale.
If the scale is subatomic,
Quantum physics is the answer.
While if it is
On a larger scale,
Classical physics is the answer.

12 yrs

Newtonian Fluid

A fluid in which
The viscous stress
From its flow, is correlated to
The local strain rates.
Water, air and alcohol
Are examples of Newtonian
Fluids but this only applies
If it is under normal circumstances.
As nearly no fluid can
Actually, fit the definition of a Newtonian Fluid
In every circumstance.

12 yrs

Thermodynamics

Matter cannot be
Created nor can
It be destroyed.
It is explained
In the first law of thermodynamics.
However, it can undergo
Changes in its form.
This does not affect
How much energy
There is; it only becomes
A different type of energy.
It is the study of how
Energy changes through time.

12 yrs

Solar Power

It won't be efficient
As regular coal
Or steam power
But it can sustain.
However, it would
Only supply a couple households.
And many rare earth
Materials such as
Lithium will need
To be mined in higher
Quantity and thus,
It wasn't as good as humans thought it was.

11 yrs

Joule's Law

Electric energy is transferred into heat energy.
It is through the resistance;
It is opposed to the persistence;
Which would mean that there is a rate in which it occurs,
With the rate not being broken,
As it does not act as a token,
As it is the electric current squared,
Times resistance and time,
It is able to make electricity rhyme,
When it comes to the conversion.
As there is a specific rate at which it occurs,
Rather than being spontaneous.

12 yrs

Uranium Dioxide

When hydrogen ends up reducing to uranium trioxide,
It can be oxidated or carbonized.
However, it can be easily converted into uranium oxide.
Uranium oxide is dangerous and radioactive;
However, it can be used as nuclear fuel.
This is naturally occurring and it can be harnessed.
This can be completely redressed.

11 yrs

Big Bang

The Big Bang created the universe.
It is what we are a product of.
It was created out of a powerful explosion.
This ended up changing atoms into elements.
It soon created many of the galaxies.
As it went on multiple sprees,
It went on its own ventures.
It created the black holes,
Which are still a mystery today.

11 yrs

Dark Matter

Much is not known about dark matter.
However, there are special properties.
Others do not have galaxy rotation curves,
Which are present in the galaxies.
They make up much of the galaxy.
However, not much is known to us.
As of right now, it is a constantly moving bus.

11 years

Steel

From workplaces to your own house,
Steel is used everywhere.
It is made of iron and carbon.
This leads to the conclusion that it is an alloy.
It is very strong as it is used in many tools.
It is combined with many other uses.
It is always made through artificial processes.
It is through the method of smelting iron ore,
That they end up reaching the end of the lore.
That is, the creation of steel.

11 yrs

Framework

Multiple APIs can come together
To form one and it
Makes an interface easier to program,
Whether it is in C to JavaScript.
And frameworks expose part
To be modified later
And soon it makes it so that.
It is easier to pull off many
Things that would not
Be possible earlier.

11 yrs

API

It makes it so it is easier
To program the target.
It increases compatibility
And it also increases many more things
Such as the speed due to
Some drivers which are sped
Up due to the compatibility layer.
Lastly, it adds many functions
That can be called upon
When it is needed.

11 yrs

Proprietary

When the software is proprietary,
It is generally for profit.
As it is a complete refit,
It is one of abolishing open source;
It is one of refitting the engine.
Propriety software denies access to the source code,
As it changes the mode.
It is weaker than open source when it comes to security,
As it is protected by copyrights.
This is because not as many can view the source;
This ends up showing the remorse.

12 yrs

Container

It is useful for IT Infrastructure
As the virtual machine will share
The same kernel while having different
IP addresses from the others.
It will run faster
Due to the drop-in resources
That are needed due to the kernel.
The kernel is being shared over multiple virtual machines
And so, it will be more efficient while
Saving computational power.

12 yrs

Linux

Linux powers many systems around the world.
It is open source;
It is one of the most secure system,
Wherein it is able to patch any bugs.
Many bugs are fixed very quickly,
Due to the nature of open-source software.
Since it can be viewed by all,
It can be compiled by all.
This means that it is possible to build a custom Linux kernel,
All from scratch.

12 yrs

C

It is the easiest programming language
To write in and it can be used
For almost everything except web development.
It has a large standard library
That can be expanded upon with
Defined functions and due to it
Being easy to learn, it is usually first taught.
It is the lowest high-level programming
Language that exists, which is why
It is used to program systems.

12 yrs

Open Source

It is a software model,
That is able to quickly change.
The open-source model is able to create its own range,
With the bounds every expanding.
Open source has the primary advantage of being more secure.
This is because the source code is seen by all,
Which causes many bugs to be fixed.
This is further combined with being able to make a clone,
Which is able to be completely customizable,
Due to changing the source code.
It has its own mode,
With the mode of thinking rejecting security by obscurity.
This is able to allow for more privacy over everything else.

12 yrs

Data & privacy

It is routed by companies,
As it is bought and sold.
They try to show it as their own mold,
With the data being breached.
There is no real privacy,
As large corporations will harvest that data,
In order to make more profit.
This has been the case since time immemorial.
True privacy can only come through using open-source software,
Though much of the hardware runs into the same problem.
It is simply not possible to solve the issue in the current system,
For it prioritizes profit over everything else.

10 yrs

Bootloaders

Bootloaders open on start
Or during booting.
They are used
To boot the kernel and the OS.
As such, it is possible
To have multiple operating systems
On the hardware with the same bootloader.
A large open source bootloader one
Is GNU GRUB.
As it is the first thing that comes up after the BIOS,
It means that if it is infected, it is necessary to replace it and rewrite the entry points,
In order to be able to restore it.
Otherwise, it will affect the rest.
Some malware goes further by affecting the BIOS,
Which are the worst headaches as it cannot easily be replaced.

10 yrs

Calculus

It is used for precision;
As well as being used with estimation.
As it employs linear approximation,
Which has the potential of estimating square roots.
The precision can be used to find speed,
Where the instantaneous values can be found.
As the ball sets off from the ground,
It is able to find the round.
This leads to the area and volume,
Wherein accurate points are found.
This is through the common application of reaching zero.
When it calculates volume of the pine,
It is able to reach the accurate measurement.
This is further combined with the tangent line,
Wherein it is able to find one property of the pine.
Which pertains to how far it is able to go,
As well as how much it can row.

11 yrs.

Statistics

As it is used for data analysis,
It utilizes standard deviation.
This is able to show the differences between data.
More specifically, it can show normality.
When it is combined with the Z-score,
It can do miracles.
It can be used for any profession,
As it can predict a recession
Or even a depression.
As it is at the center of many points,
It can be used to treat joints.
When there is a test,
It is measured with rest.

11 yrs

SISTER NIVEDITA UNIVERSITY

DG 1/2 New Town, Action Area 1, (Beside Rabindra
Tirtha), Kolkata 700156 Phone: +91 9062197986, 1800
2588 155 (Toll-Free) www.snuniv.ac.in

Professor (Dr.) Dhrubajyoti Chattopadhyay
PhD, F.A.Sc , F.Na.Sc , F.A.Sc.T
Vice Chancellor, SNU, Kolkata

Dear Readers,

The book written by Master Aritra Jana who is Thirteen years old is quite astonishing.
The poems written on Natural & Biological Sciences show his in-depth understanding
of the concepts across all the domains in Natural and Biological Sciences. It is quite
surprising that a boy who is less than thirteen years has understood the complicacies
of the various aspects of these sciences and has expressed them in a lucid format.
I believe this methodology of making students and people understand the concepts
through poems is a novel idea and can motivate a lot many younger generation to
come forward in such an initiative.

Aritra's brilliant choice of words and his justice to the rhyming sense is worth
appreciating. I wish him success in his future life and hope such a genius makes
everyone one of us proud by his contributions to the society in the form of Science &
Literature. His poems on 'Corona Virus', 'Addiction', 'Linear Motion' 'Dark Matter', 'API',
' Calculus' are really fascinating and I have enjoyed them reading.

I sincerely hope this Thirteen Year kid becomes a good person in his life and brings
a lot of valuable gifts to this society and the world at large in form of his merit and
potential that he has, in a way which will be remembered in the years to come.

Wishing all the very best!!!

Happy Reading!!!

Professor Dhrubajyoti Chattopadhyay, Ph.D., F.A.Sc, F.Na.Sc,F.A.Sc.T
Vice-Chancellor,
Sister Nivedita University
New Town, Kolkata, West Bengal 700156
Email: dhrubajyotic@gmail.com/ vc@snuniv.ac.in
Phone (M): 09831083791
Dated: 23rd September 2021

Printed in the United States
by Baker & Taylor Publisher Services